¡TRANQUILA!

Bilingual Version of Be Cool

Anger Management Group Counseling Guide with Spanish/English Activities

Written by Stephanie Lerner, MS
Certified Bilingual Educator & School Counselor

Illustrated by Michell Schalik, MA

This book is dedicated to Indrani, who taught me the invaluable anger management strategy of removing myself from the situation.

Follow Bilingual Learner on Facebook and Twitter on our pages below to see our weekly posts on developments in the ESL/counseling world and to receive our newest free/low-cost products!

www.bilinguallearner.com
www.instagram.com/bilinguallearner
www.pinterest.com/bilinguallearne
www.facebook.com/bilinguallearn
www.twitter.com/bilinguallearn

For information on this publication or others by this author, visit **www.bilinguallearner.com**
or e-mail the author at **bilinguallearner@hotmail.com**.
Special discounts are available on quantity orders.

Table of Contents

Recommendations for Running an Effective Anger Management Group

In my years as a counselor, I have found anger management groups to be the most challenging, and thus rewarding, to facilitate. This makes sense because the personality of the group often reflects the characteristics of the group theme, so the vibe in anger management groups tends to be high-energy, frustrated, strong-willed, and well…angry. For this reason, it is best to consider running an anger management group after you already have at least one year of experience in running other types of counseling groups. Despite the challenges of anger management groups, I also find them to be the most heartwarming and hilarious to facilitate! Again and again, I observe group members' eagerness and enthusiasm to do the right thing mixing uproariously with their lack of social skills—often leading to inappropriate, yet comical, comments. I remember the time years ago when a sixth-grade group member (let's call him Screech) with a huge heart but particularly weak social skills tried to bond and empathize with a fellow group member (we'll call him Zach). Zach was detailing how his anger had landed him in the school suspension room for the third time that week. Suddenly, Screech abruptly interrupted Zach with, "Hey man, I do dumba** things all the time, too!" After a startled, brief silence, I fought my urge to laugh and questioned, "Sooooo, how do we feel about that comment and language?" This turned into a teachable moment as the group agreed that the comment was well-meaning, but we needed to review the group rules. These vulnerable, bull-in-the-emotional-china-shop moments are touching in that they show how desperately group members want to do the right thing and be accepted, despite all their missteps. So, in order to manage this and help group members get the most out of the group experience, I offer the following recommendations.

- Included in this guide are eight 1-hour sessions. Each session can be easily shortened by omitting some of the activities if you have less time for group sessions or are working with younger group members. In addition, the sessions can also by lengthened by adding in some additional activities (Appendix P). Personally, I find that my group members max out at six sessions, so I generally wrap up the group experience after six sessions by skipping sessions six and seven and ending with the activities of session eight.

- In each of the sessions, appendices are referred to for facilitating the session. Immediately after the sessions guide, you will find the English appendices. Then after the English appendices, you will find the bilingual appendices which are the Spanish translations of the English appendices that the students will use. The bilingual appendices can be substituted for their English counterpart with bilingual/ESL students who need the information in Spanish. Since this is a bilingual counseling sessions guide (rather than a Spanish language counseling guide), the Spanish materials are only provided for student use; for all counselor instructions or activity descriptions, you can refer back to the English sessions or English appendices.

- Five to six members is an ideal number of group participants.

- It is best to meet once per week in a quiet, private room or area.

- This anger management curriculum was developed for group members aged 8–18 in a school setting, but it can easily be modified for use in a clinical setting.

- Additionally, if group members are too young for some of the reading/writing activities, you might modify the activities in these ways: read aloud while the group members follow along with their finger, shorten or simplify some of the lists/cards, and have group members dictate any writing activities or create a template that they can copy rather than writing on their own.

- Plan each session using the Group Notes sheet (Appendix A).

- In school settings, have a parent/guardian sign the permission form (Appendix G) for each member in your group.

- Keep a Tranquila (Be Cool) Group Binder that contains your Group Notes sheet, students' schedules/teachers, permission forms (Appendix G), and any handouts you will use.

- Both a staff and group member pre/posttest are included in this guide. There is an explanation in session one for how to administer the group member pre/posttest (Appendix B). If you work in a school setting, you can also administer the staff pre/posttest (Appendix B) to teachers who work with your group members on a daily basis. At my school, I attend weekly team meetings of all our teacher groups, and I find that this is an excellent time to fill out the staff pre/posttest. Unless you work in a school that is very relaxed and well-staffed, I recommend against just e-mailing the pre/posttests or putting them in teacher mailboxes because teachers nowadays are usually too busy to get these back to you in a timely manner. Instead, in advance of the meeting, ask for 10 minutes on the agenda from the team leader or head teacher. Then, during those 10 minutes, quickly fill out the pre/posttest with the team of teachers orally, writing down the number of their response, group-consensus-style. As you will see in Appendix B, the staff pre/posttest lends itself to this type of quick administration. I administer the staff pretest one week before the group starts and the posttest one week after the group ends. The goal is to see the numbers decrease from the pretest to the posttest.

- Demonstrate careful adherence to/reminders of Group Rules & Consequences (Appendix C) each session, and post a printout of Appendix C in the group area.

- Have scrap paper available every session for group members to use when they need to express energy and frustrations during discussion/activities. I recommend handing out the paper after the rules review so you have the undivided attention of the group during this part of the session.

- Also have warmup puzzles for group members to do as they are waiting for others to enter and the group session to start. Children in this type of group are usually high energy and can often become irritable if they have to sit around and wait for the group activities to get started. A fun and motivating puzzle is a great wait to start off the group session on a positive note. You can find entertaining anger-themed puzzle worksheets for free all over the Internet, especially at Pinterest.com. I found a few really good anger puzzles at eduBakery.com; you can access them at http://edubakery.com/Word-Scrambles/anger-management-v1-Word-Scramble (scroll to the bottom of the webpage to click on the puzzle you want, and then scroll back up to click "print"). I have not been able to find Spanish-language puzzles, though I'm sure they exist. If you are working with Spanish-speaking students, I recommend you have them color mandalas as their warmup (you can find lots of free mandalas at Pinterest.com).

- Use the group members' responses to the Group Evaluation (Appendix E) each week to plan/adapt your next session. I laminate and hang Appendix E as a poster so we can refer to it at the end of every session.

- During the first few minutes of a session, as group members trickle in, ask if anyone wants to discuss anything on their mind or from the previous week. In school settings, this is also a good time to address any discipline problems related to anger issues that might have occurred with a group member in the last week. Try to keep these discussions to no more than 5–10 minutes so as to not focus the entire session on them. If you feel that group members will have trouble staying within this time constraint, post the following guidelines on chart paper and review them with group members each session, as needed. A Spanish language version of these guidelines can be found in Appendix SP.

  Tranquila (Be Cool) discussions are:

  - 5–10 minutes (we will set our group timer)

  - focused on solutions, not problems

  - not name specific

  - helpful

  - serious

  - about anger management issues

- During the beginning of each session, it is good to review the optional homework assignment if you gave one during the previous session. Session homework is important because it gets group members to apply the skills they have learned and practiced in group. Application is an effective way to transfer information from our short-term memory into long-term memory, where we want group members to keep their Tranquila (Be Cool) skills. Also, utilizing the homework feature and following up with it in subsequent sessions helps to ensure that the skills learned in group are reviewed and discussed in multiple sessions, rather than just covered in a single session. However, this review is optional, so you can skip it if the group session runs long and there is no time.

- There are a lot of read-aloud and sharing opportunities in these sessions. Always make sure to remind group members that they can say "pass" anytime they do not want to read aloud or share.

- Sometimes group members are resistant to participating in role-play exercises. It is important to get everyone involved in role-playing so they can practice their anger management skills in a safe, non-angry environment. Here are some ways to get resistant group members involved in role-playing:

  - Tell group members they will vote on the best role-playing at the end of the group session and that all the actors in the role-playing skit that receives the most votes will get a prize.

  - Try giving resistant group members pre-written role-playing skits that highlight their particular anger management strategy so they can read aloud and follow their lines. This allows them to focus on practicing their strategy without the distraction of having to think through and act out an improvisation.

  - Another option is to spend a session or two substituting video skits or public service announcements (PSAs) for the role-playing activity until group members get more comfortable with each other and the group experience. For this to be effective, the video clips must show other people using or discussing anger management strategies. See the additional activities (Appendix P) at the end of this guide if you would like more information on video skits or PSAs. At the time of this printing, there are no free Spanish language video skits or public service announcements (PSAs) on anger management that show how other people manage their anger in a healthful way. Instead you can type Angry Birds Spanish into an internet search engine and take your pick of various Spanish language cartoons showing the popular characters dealing with anger in both healthful and unhealthful ways.

  – If your entire group is uncomfortable with role-playing, it is crucial to spend 5–10 minutes during that session or during the following session discussing what is causing their discomfort. Then spend an additional 10–15 minutes guiding them to the idea that practicing their anger management strategies in a safe, non-angry situation is necessary in order to achieve what they want for themselves: calming their anger in real-life, stressful situations. During this discussion, it is helpful to address how practice situations may feel silly but give us the skills we need to calm ourselves when the stress or conflict is overwhelming. Liken their anger role-playing group practice to how it might feel lining up outside a perfectly safe building on a rainy day for a fire drill. You might also give group members the analogy of a professional athlete's practice leading up to game day; discuss how every professional athlete must spend hours practicing against his/her own teammates each day to prepare for that one- or two-hour game against the competing athlete(s) on game day.

  – If you have one group member for whom none of the above strategies works, you can tell that them that they may skip role-playing during this one session but that they must participate in the role-playing exercise next week. If the group member can't agree to this, meet with them privately after group to explore the reason and find a solution. If no solution can be found, it is probably better to work with the group member in individual sessions where there is more flexibility and privacy in helping them learn anger management skills.

• For group members who have a disciplinary referral/problem that relates to their anger management strategy, it may be best to set up an individual session to facilitate more intensive role-playing so they can practice applying their strategy to the disciplinary referral/problem situation. In these cases, have the group member repeatedly apply their anger management strategy to the referral/problem situation, which you recreate for them. For example, if the group member had a problem with blowing up at someone kicking their chair, I might kick their chair while they practice using their strategy instead of blowing up.

• When time allows, play the game Cool It! (Appendix N) for about 5–10 minutes at the end of each session. This game leaves the group members with a positive feeling about the group so that they look forward to attending the next session. In addition, the game helps them to become familiar with each of the anger management strategies.

• I find that collecting group data helps me to improve future groups and promote my program with school stakeholders (parents/administrators/staff). In Appendix M, I have included an extensive six-part data plan that allows you to present all aspects of your group's successes to counseling program stakeholders. Alternately, you can also compile and present as few of the parts as you want because data analysis and compilation can be time consuming. I have found that one of the biggest challenges in compiling and presenting data is actually getting anyone to look at it! Everyone always has more e-mails than they can read in a day, and unfortunately an e-mail on a bland topic like data will usually get overlooked. For that reason, I take all identifying group member information off my data and then post it in high-traffic, staff-only areas such as the staff bathroom (and usually on the wall right in front of the commode; it might sound a bit unseemly, but it works!). Since I started posting data in the bathroom, I actually have colleagues and administrators tell me varying versions of, "you know, I was in the bathroom looking at your data and I never realized that 60% of students' grades went up during your group" or "I was so impressed that Han Solo actually had 22 disciplinary referrals before your group and only 3 after!" Some other high-traffic areas to post your data might include: right above or on the photocopy machine, on the fridge right by the handle in the staff lunch room, or next to staff mailboxes.

- If group members will need school passes to attend your group, here are some easy steps for making passes:

    - Get two copies of the student's schedule.

    - Cut/tape these copies together with the pass in Appendix O attached.

    - On colorful paper, photocopy half the number of passes you will need for this student, and cut the copies in half.

    - Repeat the three steps above for all other group members.

    - Paperclip a stack of passes together for each session, with one pass for each group member.

    - Hand out one paper-clipped stack on the day of the group session.

- I often have a follow-up session about a month or two after the group ends to check in on group members' experiences/successes with anger management. To do this, I send group members a photocopy of their last anger management strategy note card one week before the follow-up group so they can have a reminder to practice it. Then, during the follow-up session, I generally repeat the session five steps. At this time, I also compile and analyze the After Group data (Appendix M).

- I have included an appendix with suggestions for additional activities (Appendix P) if you'd like to extend the length of your individual group sessions past 1 hour or if you'd like to have more than eight sessions. You can also substitute any of the additional activities for a particular session activity if that activity won't work with your group member population.

American School Counselor Association National Standards

The American School Counselor Association (ASCA) sets the national framework for a model school counseling program. As a result, the Tranquila (Be Cool) session activities are aligned with the following ASCA competencies and indicators that fall under the Personal/Social domain.

Personal/Social Development: ASCA National Standards for personal/social development guide school counseling programs to provide the foundation for personal and social growth as students progress through school and into adulthood.

Standard A: Students will acquire the knowledge, attitudes and interpersonal skills to help them understand and respect self and others.

PS:A1   Acquire Self-knowledge
PS:A1.1   Develop positive attitudes toward self as a unique and worthy person
PS:A1.2   Identify values, attitudes and beliefs
PS:A1.3   Learn the goal-setting process
PS:A1.4   Understand change is a part of growth
PS:A1.5   Identify and express feelings
PS:A1.6   Distinguish between appropriate and inappropriate behavior
PS:A1.7   Recognize personal boundaries, rights and privacy needs
PS:A1.8   Understand the need for self-control and how to practice it
PS:A1.9   Demonstrate cooperative behavior in groups
PS:A1.10   Identify personal strengths and assets

PS:A2   Acquire Interpersonal Skills
PS:A2.1   Recognize that everyone has rights and responsibilities
PS:A2.2   Respect alternative points of view
PS:A2.3   Recognize, accept, respect and appreciate individual differences
PS:A2.4   Recognize, accept and appreciate ethnic and cultural diversity
PS:A2.6   Use effective communications skills
PS:A2.7   Know that communication involves speaking, listening and non-verbal behavior

Standard B: Students will make decisions, set goals and take necessary action to achieve goals.

PS:B1   Self-knowledge Application
PS:B1.1   Use a decision-making and problem-solving model
PS:B1.2   Understand consequences of decisions and choices
PS:B1.3   Identify alternative solutions to a problem
PS:B1.4   Develop effective coping skills for dealing with problems
PS:B1.5   Demonstrate when, where and how to seek help for solving problems and making decisions
PS:B1.6   Know how to apply conflict resolution skills
PS:B1.7   Demonstrate a respect and appreciation for individual and cultural differences
PS:B1.9   Identify long- and short-term goals
PS:B1.10   Identify alternative ways of achieving goals
PS:B1.11   Use persistence and perseverance in acquiring knowledge and skills
PS:B1.12   Develop an action plan to set and achieve realistic goals

Standard C: Students will understand safety and survival skills.

PS:C1   Acquire Personal Safety Skills

PS:C1.3   Learn about the differences between appropriate and inappropriate physical contact

PS:C1.4   Demonstrate the ability to set boundaries, rights and personal privacy

PS:C1.6   Identify resource people in the school and community, and know how to seek their help

PS:C1.7   Apply effective problem-solving and decision-making skills to make safe and healthy choices

PS:C1.9   Learn how to cope with peer pressure

PS:C1.10   Learn techniques for managing stress and conflict

Tranquila (Be Cool) Anger Management Group Counseling Sessions

 ## Session One

Objectives

The group member will:

- Make introductions with other members
- Identify the purpose of the group
- Discuss group rules/norms
- Identify some basic tips/strategies related to anger management

Materials

- Appendices A/B/C/D/E/I, scrap paper, pencils

Activities

1. Take attendance (Appendix A). It's good to provide a warmup activity (Appendix I) for prompt group members; other members often trickle in slowly during the beginning of the first group session because it's a new routine for them.

2. Tell group members that the purpose of the group is to learn and practice ways to calm their anger and express it in healthful ways. Show the rules poster (Appendix C), and have each group member read a rule aloud and share what he/she thinks the rule means. Remember to always remind group members that they can say "pass" if they do not want to read aloud or share. Additionally, as mentioned in the recommendations section, it's always good to have scrap paper available in every session for group members to use when they need to express energy and frustrations. I recommend handing out the paper after the rules review so you have the undivided attention of the group during this part of the session.

3. Have students introduce themselves by giving their name, grade, and favorite calming activity. You should go first to model this for group members.

4. Hand out the group member pretest (Appendix B), and read aloud as group members fill in Yes/No for each statement. Collect and save these pretests until the last group session.

5. Hand out an Anger Tips sheet to each group member (Appendix D) and read it in a round-robin fashion. You can also add a movement aspect to this activity, which is often needed by group members struggling with anger issues. Let group members actively show their response to the "Anger Tips" by stepping forward if they think an Important Anger Fact is true and standing still if

they think the fact is false; in the same vein, members can step forward if they've tried a Managing Anger strategy or stand still if they haven't tried it. After the group has finished reading, ask group members on which tips they need further explanation. Group members should take these sheets home to share with family and display in a prominent place.

6. Optional Homework Activity: Instruct group members to do the following, "As you're spending time with people over the next week, notice what things you're doing to handle your anger if you get mad. Think about what works best to calm you down when you're angry. We'll talk about this during the next session."

7. Complete the group evaluation (Appendix E). To do this, read each evaluation statement aloud while group members hold up fingers to indicate whether they agree with/disagree with/feel "sort of" about each statement. Then tally group members' responses in each Agree/Sort of/Disagree column (on the Group Notes sheet in Appendix A) for use in planning the next session.

Session Two

Objectives

The group member will:

- Learn about nine anger management strategies and choose the one that works best for them
- Role-play their chosen anger management strategy

Materials

- Appendices A/C/E/F/H, note cards, scrap paper, pencils

Activities

1. Take attendance (Appendix A). Ask group members whether there is anything they want to discuss relating to anger management issues; guide them to limit responses/discussions to 5–10 minutes (see the recommendations section for tips on keeping within these time constraints).

2. Show the rules poster (Appendix C), and have each group member read a rule aloud. Remember to always remind group members that they can say "pass" if they do not want to read aloud.

3. Ask group members to share what things calmed them down when they felt angry over the last week. Hand out an Anger Management Strategies sheet to each group member (Appendix F) and read it in a round-robin fashion. After the group has finished reading, ask group members on which numbers they need further explanation.

4. Group members should pick their favorite anger management strategy from Appendix F and write it on a note card, using the goal prompt from Appendix H. You should model this first by using the prompt to copy your favorite anger management strategy on a note card.

5. Each group member reads their anger management strategy note card aloud to the group.

6. Each group member role-plays the anger management strategy on their note card, with you acting as the instigator (who/what) who makes that student angry. For example, ask "Who wants to practice their strategy with me?" Then ask the volunteering group member, "What makes you angry at school?" If the group member says, "Kids who kick my chair make me angry," then gently kick the group member's chair while coaching them to act out the anger management strategy on their note card.

7. Collects the note cards and Anger Management Strategies sheets. (Photocopy the note cards after group and give the originals to group members as a reminder to practice their preferred anger management strategy during the week. Keep the photocopies for the next group session.) Praise group members for their efforts.

8. Optional Homework Activity: Instruct group members to do the following, "As you're spending time with people over the next week, practice your chosen anger management strategy when you feel mad. Pay attention to how/whether your strategy calms you down and keeps you out of trouble. We'll talk about this during the next session."

9. Complete the group evaluation (Appendix E). To do this, read each evaluation statement aloud while group members hold up fingers to indicate whether they agree with/disagree with/feel "sort of" about each statement. Then tally group members' responses in each Agree/Sort of/Disagree column (on the Group Notes sheet in Appendix A) for use in planning the next session.

Session Three

Objectives

The group member will:

- Role-play their chosen anger management strategy
- Discuss their success with their anger management strategy
- Learn that anger can cause illnesses

Materials

- Appendices A/C/E/F/H/J/N, note cards, scrap paper, pencils

Activities

1. Take attendance (Appendix A). Ask group members whether there is anything they want to discuss relating to anger management issues; guide them to limit responses/discussions to 5–10 minutes (see the recommendations section for tips on keeping within these time constraints).

2. Show the rules poster (Appendix C), and have each group member read a rule aloud. Remember to always remind group members that they can say "pass" if they do not want to read aloud.

3. Read "Anger Causes Illness" from Appendix J and discuss briefly.

4. Hand out the photocopies of the anger management strategy note cards and Anger Management Strategies sheets (Appendix F) from the last session. Have group members read Appendix F aloud in a round-robin fashion to review.

5. Show group members the Goal Success Sharing Steps (Appendix H) and model how to do steps 1 and 2. For example, you can read off, "When I'm angry, I promise to try to use an 'I' message to talk it out" from your anger management strategy note card from the last session. Then you can tell group, "When my sister told me that I didn't cook a tasty dinner, I told her 'I feel sad and unappreciated when you tell me that the dinner I worked hard to cook isn't tasty.'"

6. Give group members 1 minute to think of a success they had in the past week with the anger management strategy on their note card.

7. Allow each group member to present the steps in Appendix H to the group. Ask group members if they feel their anger management strategy is working to calm their anger or if they need to pick a different strategy (Appendix F).

8. Group members write their strategy from Appendix F on a new note card OR pick a different way to handle anger from Appendix F and write it on a new note card, using the goal prompt from Appendix H. You should model this first by using the prompt to copy your favorite anger management strategy on a note card.

9. Each group member reads their anger management strategy note card aloud to the group.

10. Each group member role-plays the anger management strategy on their note card, with you acting as the instigator (who/what) who makes that group member angry (see session two for an example of this, if necessary). Because this session may run long, it is fine to have half the group do their role-playing today and the other half do their role-playing during the next session.

11. Collect the note cards and Anger Management Strategies sheets. (Photocopy the note cards after group and give the originals to group members as a reminder to practice their preferred anger management strategy during the week. Keep the photocopies for the next group session.)

12. Optional Homework Activity: Instruct group members to do the following, "Talk to your family about the anger management strategy you're using. Tell them how it's working for you, and ask them what strategy calms them down. We'll talk about this during the next session."

13. If there is time, Play Cool It! (Appendix N) with group members.

14. Complete the group evaluation (Appendix E). To do this, read each evaluation statement aloud while group members hold up fingers to indicate whether they agree with/disagree with/feel "sort of" about each statement. Then tally group members' responses in each Agree/Sort of/Disagree column (on the Group Notes sheet in Appendix A) for use in planning the next session.

Session Four

Objectives

The group member will:

- Role-play their chosen anger management strategy

- Discuss their success with their anger management strategy

- Learn that their thoughts cause their anger

Materials

- Appendices A/C/E/F/H/J/N, note cards, scrap paper, pencils

Activities

1. Take attendance (Appendix A). Ask group members whether there's anything they want to discuss relating to anger management issues; guide them to limit responses/discussions to 5–10 minutes (see the recommendations section for tips on keeping within these time constraints).

2. Show the rules poster (Appendix C) and have each group member read a rule aloud. Ask group members to share the highlights of their discussion with family members about their preferred anger management strategies.

3. Read "What Causes Your Anger?" from Appendix J and discuss briefly.

4. Hand out the photocopies of the anger management strategy note cards and Anger Management Strategies sheets (Appendix F) from the last session. Briefly review Appendix F with group members.

5. Show group members the Goal Success Sharing Steps (Appendix H) and model how to do steps 1 and 2. For an example of this modeling, see session three.

6. Give group members 1 minute to think of a success they had in the past week with the anger management strategy on their note card.

7. Allow each group member to present the steps in Appendix H to the group.

8. Group members write their strategy from Appendix F on a new note card OR pick a different way to handle anger from Appendix F and write it on a new note card, using the goal prompt from Appendix H. You should model this first by using the prompt to copy your favorite anger management strategy on a note card.

9. Each group member reads their anger management strategy note card aloud to the group.

10. Each group member role-plays the anger management strategy on their note card, with you acting as the instigator (who/what) who makes that group member angry (see session two for an example of this, if necessary). Alternately, if you feel group members are ready and can handle this, you can teach them how to role-play in pairs. Be very careful, making sure that group members clearly understand how to choose a less-upsetting anger stimulus and to act it out gently as the instigator.

To teach them to role-play with a partner, you can select one generic anger stimulus (for example, giving mean looks or pointing without touching) and then have each pair role-play for the group while you carefully monitor their interaction. *If this group session runs long, it is fine to just role-play with the group members who didn't get to role-play last week.*

11. Collect the note cards and Anger Management Strategies sheets. (Photocopy the note cards after group and give the originals to group members as a reminder to practice their preferred anger management strategy during the week. Keep the photocopies for the next group session.)

12. Optional Homework Activity: Instruct group members to do the following, "Share the information you learned from the reading 'What Causes Your Anger' with a family member. We'll talk about this during the next session."

13. If there is time, play Cool It! (Appendix N) with group members.

14. Complete the group evaluation (Appendix E). To do this, read each evaluation statement aloud while group members hold up fingers to indicate whether they agree with/disagree with/feel "sort of" about each statement. Then tally group members' responses in each Agree/Sort of/Disagree column (on the Group Notes sheet in Appendix A) for use in planning the next session.

Session Five

Objectives

The group member will:

- Role-play their chosen anger management strategy
- Discuss their success with their anger management strategy

Materials

- Appendices A/C/E/F/H/N, note cards, scrap paper, pencils

Activities

1. Take attendance (Appendix A). Ask group members whether there is anything they want to discuss relating to anger management issues; guide them to limit responses/discussions to 5–10 minutes.

2. Show the rules poster (Appendix C), and have each group member read a rule aloud. Remember to always remind group members that they can say "pass" if they do not want to read aloud.

3. Ask group members to share their family members' reactions to "What Causes Your Anger?" Ask them, "What makes you angry?" to which they should all answer: "your thoughts." Prompt this answer from last session's reading, if necessary. Hand out the photocopies of the anger management strategy note cards and Anger Management Strategies sheets (Appendix F) from the last session.

4. Show group members the Goal Success Sharing Steps (Appendix H) and model how to do steps 1 and 2. For an example of this modeling, see session three.

5. Give group members 1 minute to think of a success they had in the past week with the anger management strategy on their note card.

6. Allow each group member to present the steps in Appendix H to the group.

7. Group members write their strategy from Appendix F on a new note card OR pick a different way to handle anger from Appendix F and write it on a new note card, using the goal prompt from Appendix H. You should model this first by using the prompt to copy your favorite anger management strategy on a note card.

8. Each group member reads their anger management strategy note card aloud to the group.

9. Each group member role-plays the anger management strategy on their note card, with you acting as the instigator (who/what) who makes that group member angry (see session two for an example of this, if necessary). Alternately, if you feel group members are ready and can handle this, you can teach them how to role-play in pairs. See session four if you need tips on this.

10. Collect the note cards and Anger Management Strategies sheets. (Photocopy the note cards after group and give the originals to group members as a reminder to practice their preferred anger management strategy during the week. Keep the photocopies for the next group session).

---

11. Optional Homework Activity: Instruct group members to do the following, "Ask a friend to tell you about any changes they have seen in you since you started the Tranquila (Be Cool) group. We'll talk about this during the next session."

12. If there is time, Play Cool It! (Appendix N) with group members.

13. Complete the group evaluation (Appendix E). To do this, read each evaluation statement aloud while and group members hold up fingers to indicate whether they agree with/disagree with/feel "sort of" about each statement. Then tally group members' responses in each Agree/Sort of/Disagree column (on the Group Notes sheet in Appendix A) for use in planning the next session.

Session Six

Objectives

The group member will:

- Complete an art project that shows their chosen anger management strategy applied to their anger triggers

- Gain the insight that using their anger management strategy can influence others' behavior

- Discuss their success with their anger management strategy

Materials

- Appendices A/C/E/F/H, note cards, scrap paper, drawing paper, crayons or markers, pencils

Activities

1. Take attendance (Appendix A). Ask group members whether there is anything they want to discuss relating to anger management issues; guide them to limit responses/discussions to 5–10 minutes.

2. Show the rules poster (Appendix C), and have each group member read a rule aloud. Remember to always remind group members that they can say "pass" if they do not want to read aloud.

3. Ask each group member to share their friend's observations of how they have changed since starting the Tranquila (Be Cool) group. Briefly discuss the cyclical nature of behavior change—that when we change our own behavior, others around us react to this and change their behavior. You might give group members the following example: if a student with discipline problems starts to follow the rules in class and starts being nicer to the teacher, the teacher will start to change their behavior toward the student (for example, no longer getting mad at the student because the student is no longer breaking any rules or being rude).

4. Hand out the photocopies of the anger management strategy note cards and Anger Management Strategies sheets (Appendix F) from the last session. Have a group member model steps 1 and 2 of the Goal Success Sharing Steps (Appendix H). Allow each group member to share their goal success by presenting the steps in Appendix H to the group. If anyone wants to change their anger management strategy, have them write their new strategy on a new note card, using the goal prompt from Appendix H. For all group members keeping the same anger management strategy, just collect their old note cards after finishing the art project below.

5. Have group members complete the following art project. Hand out blank paper to group members and tell them to draw themselves in an ocean on top of a wave of anger. They should write whatever it is that makes them mad inside the wave. Then they should write their anger management strategy next to themselves on the wave. Discuss with group members the importance of staying on top of and managing their anger like they would ride on top of a wave. Discuss the alternative, which is letting their anger control and crash over them just like the wave would if they don't stay on top of it. Make sure to first model a drawing showing your anger triggers and anger management strategy (see example drawing below) so group members

understand how to complete the drawing. After everyone finishes, let group members present their drawings and share what anger management strategy they use to ride their anger wave.

6. If there is time, have group members role-play the anger management strategy on their note card, working in pairs. See session four if you need tips on this.

7. Collect the note cards and Anger Management Strategies sheets. (Photocopy the note cards after group and give the originals to group members as a reminder to practice their preferred anger management strategy during the week. Keep the photocopies for the next group session).

8. Optional Homework Activity: Instruct group members to do the following, "We discussed how our changes in behavior cause others to change their behavior. Over the next week, watch your teachers, parents, or peers to see if using your anger strategy has caused others to change. We'll talk about this during the next session."

9. Complete the group evaluation (Appendix E). To do this, read each evaluation statement aloud while group members hold up fingers to indicate whether they agree with/disagree with/feel "sort of" about each statement. Then tally group members' responses in each Agree/Sort of/Disagree column (on the Group Notes sheet in Appendix A) for use in planning the next session.

 **Session Seven**

Objectives

The group member will:

- Apply their knowledge of anger management strategies by advising other group members on how to manage their anger

- Discuss their success with their anger management strategy

Materials

- Appendices A/C/E/F/H/K/N, note cards, scrap paper, pencils

Activities

1. Take attendance (Appendix A). Ask group members whether there is anything they want to discuss relating to anger management issues; guide them to limit responses/discussions to 5–10 minutes. Discuss with the group that the next session will be the last scheduled session. Tell group members that they can meet with you individually on an as-needed basis and give them the procedures for requesting this. In addition, ask them whether they would like a follow-up group session in one month and if so, schedule it. See the recommendations section at the beginning of this guide for tips and suggested content for the follow-up session.

2. Show the rules poster (Appendix C), and have each group member read a rule aloud. Remember to always remind group members that they can say "pass" if they do not want to read aloud.

3. Ask group members to share their own observations of how others' behaviors toward them have changed since they started the Tranquila (Be Cool) group. Again, briefly review the cyclical nature of behavior change—that when we change our own behavior, others around us react to this and change their behavior.

4. Hand out the photocopies of the anger management strategy note cards and Anger Management Strategies sheets (Appendix F) from the last session. Have a group member model steps 1 and 2 of the Goal Success Sharing Steps (Appendix H). Allow each group member to share their goal success by presenting the steps in Appendix H to the group. If anyone wants to change their anger management strategy, have them write their new strategy on a new note card, using the goal prompt from Appendix H. For all group members keeping the same anger management strategy, just collect their old note cards after finishing the Dear Be Cool Experts activity below.

5. Tell the group that because they are now experts on anger management strategies, they will have a chance today to advise other group members on anger issues. Pair up group members and hand out an anger scenario from Dear Tranquila (Be Cool) Experts (Appendix K) to each pair. Give pairs 5–10 minutes to use their red Anger Management Strategies sheets (Appendix F), as well as their own ideas, to find a solution for their fellow anger sufferer. Then have each pair read their anger scenario aloud and tell the group what advice they would give to the writer to solve the anger problem.

6. Collect the note cards and Anger Management Strategies sheets. (Photocopy the note cards after group and give the originals to group members as a reminder to practice their preferred anger management strategy during the week. Keep the photocopies for the next group session).

7. Optional Homework Activity: Instruct group members to do the following, "We've used our red Anger Management Strategies sheets a lot in this group to find the best anger management strategies for ourselves. Now that our group is ending soon, we need to find a way to keep reviewing this sheet so we keep practicing our anger strategies. Think about how you'll remember to use your Anger Management Strategies sheet during difficult times. For example, you might keep it on the bedside table to read each night before bed, post it on the bathroom mirror to read each morning while brushing your teeth, or put it in your smartphone as a daily reminder. We'll talk about this during the next session."

8. Let group members vote on whether they'd like to play the Cool It! game (Appendix N) or role-play their anger management strategy. Proceed with the activity that the group chooses. Alternately, if group members would like to try something new, you can substitute one of the additional activities (Appendix P) for the Cool It! game or the role-playing activity.

9. Complete the group evaluation (Appendix E). To do this, read each evaluation statement aloud while group members hold up fingers to indicate whether they agree with/disagree with/feel "sort of" about each statement. Then tally group members' responses in each Agree/Sort of/Disagree column (on the Group Notes sheet in Appendix A) for use in planning the next session.

Session Eight

Objectives

The group member will:

- Reflect on their learnings/experiences with group

- Evaluate the group experience

- Discuss their success with their anger management strategy

Materials

- Appendices A/B (with pretests completed from session one)/C/F/H/L/N, scrap paper, chart paper, pencils

Activities

1. Take attendance (Appendix A). Ask group members whether there is anything they want to discuss relating to anger management issues; guide them to limit responses/discussions to 5–10 minutes.

2. Show the rules poster (Appendix C), and have each group member read a rule aloud. Remember to always remind group members that they can say "pass" if they do not want to read aloud. Remind the group that this is the last group session, and briefly discuss plans for the follow-up session, if you will be having one.

3. Ask group members to share their ideas about what they will do with their red Anger Management Strategies sheet so that they remember to use their chosen anger management strategy during difficult times. Ask group members a final time, "What makes you angry?" to which they should all answer: "your thoughts." Hand out the photocopies of the anger management strategy note cards and Anger Management Strategies sheets (Appendix F) from the last session; group members can take the sheets home with them at the end of the session. Have a group member model steps 1 and 2 of the Goal Success Sharing Steps (Appendix H). Allow each group member to share their goal success by presenting the steps in Appendix H to the group. If anyone wants to change their anger management strategy, have them write their new strategy on a new note card, using the goal prompt from Appendix H. Group members can take their note cards home with them at the end of the session unless you need to make photocopies for a follow-up session.

4. Review with group members all the main points learned during the Tranquila (Be Cool) sessions. To best facilitate this review, give group members 1 minute to think of the main things they learned in group, then write have them share their ideas while you write their responses on chart paper.

5. Hand out the group member pretest/posttest (Appendix B) and read it aloud as group members fill in Yes/No for each posttest statement. Make sure group members write answers in the posttest column and don't change any of their pretest answers. Collect and save the completed posttests for data purposes.

---

6. Complete the Group Experience Evaluation (Appendix L). To do this, read each evaluation statement aloud while group members write down their response to that statement. Collect and retain the completed evaluations for data purposes.

7. Play Cool It! (Appendix N) one last time with group members.

8. Praise the group members for all of their hard work. Ask whether there is anything more they would like to discuss or any other help they need. Remind them to let you know if they need to meet with you anytime in the future.

 # Appendix A: Group Notes

Group Name: _____ **Session #:** ____ **Date:** _____

Activities:

Summary of Session:

Group Member	Attended?	Questions & Points to Work on/Discuss	Teacher Comments

Session Critique by Group Members:

Behaviors	Agree – 3	Sort of – 2	Disagree – 1
The group leader only talked a little.			
The group members listened to me.			
What we did/discussed was important/helpful to me.			
I hope we do the same kind of things next time.			

 Appendix B: Pre/Posttests

Group Member Pre/Posttest

Name: _____ Date: _____

BE COOL! GROUP

PRETEST: YES or NO	Statements/Questions	POSTTEST: YES or NO
	I can control my anger.	
	I know five calming anger strategies.	
	Anger is a normal human feeling.	
	Other people or events can make me angry.	
	Anger can cause heart problems/disease.	

Staff Pre/Posttest

Administer this pre/posttest orally to the group members' teacher/group of teachers; the pretest can be administered one week before the group begins, and the posttest can be administered one week after the group ends. Use the scale below to write a numbered answer to each question. Make additional copies of this page if you have more than five group members.

- 1 = You see the student/client exhibit the behavior rarely or never
- 2 = You see the student/client exhibit the behavior monthly
- 3 = You see the student/client exhibit the behavior weekly
- 4 = You see the student/client exhibit the behavior daily
- NA = not applicable

Name of Student	How often does he/she express anger by assaulting people or objects?	How often does he/she express anger through criticism, sarcasm, insults, or profanity?	How often is he/she unable to reduce or control his/her level of anger?	How often do his/her angry outbursts interfere with relationships with peers/staff?	How often is he/she unable to follow directions?	How often is he/she unable to complete schoolwork?
1._____ Pretest Posttest						
2._____ Pretest Posttest						
3._____ Pretest Posttest						
4._____ Pretest Posttest						
5._____ Pretest Posttest						
6._____ Pretest Posttest						

 # Appendix C: Group Rules & Consequences

Group Rules

1. Only say helpful comments.

2. Don't tell others what is said in the group.

3. One person talks at a time; there are no side conversations.

4. Use the bathroom before or after group only.

5. Name-calling is not allowed.

6. Don't touch someone else's stuff.

7. If you arrive late, bring a pass with the time/an adult signature.

Consequences

1. Private warning

2. Removal from group

 Appendix D: Anger Tips

 ## Important Anger Facts

- Anger is a normal human response, and everyone has it.

- Problems come from unhealthy ways of expressing anger.

- Feeling sick or tired makes it easy to get angry.

- YOUR THOUGHTS make you angry, not other people or events.

- The best time to control your anger is when it begins.

- If you don't control your anger, it can get worse.

- People can hurt themselves/others when they get mad.

 ## Managing Anger

- Tell someone how you feel.

- Relax and take deep breaths.

- Get away from the situation that is making you angry.

- Exercise to burn off your anger.

- Know you have a choice in how you express anger; think of the different choices you have.

- Know your choice will lead to a consequence; think of the consequences of what you do.

 ## You Will Have Problems if You

- **Break something**

- **Hit or kick people or animals**

- **Yell in anger**

- **Break rules at school/work or home**

 # Appendix E: Group Evaluation

Behaviors	Agree – 3	Sort of – 2	Disagree – 1
The group leader only talked a little.			
The group members listened to me.			
What we did was important and helpful.			
I hope we do the same kind of things next session.			

 # Appendix F: Anger Management Strategies

For best results, copy Appendix F on red cardstock because group members will use it each session. After each session, collect the photocopies of this appendix and pass them out again in the following session.

HOW DO YOU HANDLE YOUR ANGER??

Circle the anger management strategy that will work best for YOU!

1. Take time out and relax.
Count to ten. Take five deep breaths. Feel yourself go all rubbery.

2. Walk away from the problem.
Go to a safe place.

3. Write or draw your feelings on paper.
Make angry pictures or words showing how you feel.

4. Use humor. Make a joke out of it.
Think of something funny about what happened or laugh at yourself.

5. Think: it's no big deal. Convince yourself to LET IT GO!
Decide if the problem is worth getting upset over.

6. Talk it out. Use "I" messages.
Tell the person/group how you feel OR tell them to stop in a serious way.

7. Say you are sorry and make up.
Only do this if you really mean it.

8. Get help from an adult.
Or ask another student to mediate.

9. Make a list of bad consequences of you getting angry.
Read the list to calm yourself and control your anger.

 # Appendix G: Parent Permission Letter

Date: _____

Dear Parent:

The Comprehensive School Counseling Program at _____ School includes the opportunity for students to participate in small group counseling sessions. Your child _____, has been referred for participation in school counseling. With your permission, your child will be seen on a scheduled basis at school by the school counselor. These group sessions will focus on the topic of _____.
The sessions will not detract from your child's academic program. Please note that participation in the group is completely voluntary, and confidentiality will be addressed and respected.

The school counselor assigned to your child is _____.

It is frequently beneficial and necessary for the school counselor and school-based staff (principal, assistant principal, social worker, psychologist, teacher, nurse, etc.) to exchange information about your child (goals, strategies, progress, etc.). All communication will take place on an as-needed basis and will focus appropriately on the needs of your child.

This permission is effective for the school year _____.

If you would like for your child to have small group sessions with the school counselor, please sign and return this form to the counseling office. If you have any questions or concerns, feel free to call _____.

Thank you,

_____
School Counselor

I give my permission for _____ **to participate in small group counseling sessions with the school counselor.**

_____
Parent Signature

_____
Phone Number

 # Appendix H: Goal Prompt Template & Goal Success Sharing Steps

For best results, copy the Goal Prompt and Goal Success Sharing Steps on a large, laminated, colored piece of paper because it will be hung on the wall for group members to use as a model in every session.

Goal Prompt:

When I'm angry, I promise to try to:

_____.

Goal Success Sharing Steps:

1. Read your goal aloud.

2. Give an example of your success with the goal.

 # Appendix I: Draw Your Anger Warmup

A warmup puzzle is a great way to start off the group session on a positive note. I recommend providing an optional warmup puzzle worksheet for group members at the beginning of every session. You can find really good anger-themed puzzle worksheets for free all over the Internet, especially at Pinterest.com. I found a few really good anger puzzles at eduBakery.com; you can access them at http://edubakery.com/Word-Scrambles/anger-management-v1-Word-Scramble (scroll to the bottom of the webpage to click on the puzzle you want, and then scroll back up to click "print"). Here is one of my own warmups to start you off....

When you're angry, you feel one way. Then when your mood changes and you're feeling calm, you feel a different way. Draw a picture below showing your anger feeling and your calm feeling.

ANGER: Draw a picture of it in the box above.   **CALM: Draw a picture of it in the box above.**

 # Appendix J: Anger Informational Readings

Anger Causes Illness

Anger is a normal human feeling that all people have. When people limit their angry responses and express anger calmly, it can actually be a very useful emotion. But did you know that getting angry a lot can hurt the inside of your body?? Now we're not talking about stubbing your toe when you kick something in anger or getting a bloody nose if you are in a fight—we all KNOW of those ways that anger can hurt us. But, did you know that feeling angry repeatedly for long periods of time can damage your heart, your stomach, and your intestines; increase your blood pressure, etc.? There have been many studies throughout the world in the last 100 years showing that people who are more angry have more health problems. Specific studies have shown that angry people are twice as likely to develop heart disease and have higher rates of cancer. One of the reasons for this is that people have increases in blood pressure and heart rate when they are angry, and our bodies can't handle these increases if they happen too often. Another reason for this is that anger and stress can lead to inflammation that, over many years, can cause cancer. So even if you aren't getting in trouble at school/work, or fighting with people, your body, your health, and your HEART are still suffering from anger!

What Causes Your Anger?

So, what causes YOU to get angry? Is it: Your friends? Your teachers? Hard schoolwork? Your parents? Your brother or sister? Mean looks? When someone yells at you?

The answer is NO! None of the things above can make you angry; only you can make yourself angry. You might think that sounds crazy, but let's look at an example. Imagine that one day you're waiting quietly outside your teacher's door for the bell to ring. You're minding your own business, not bothering anyone. All of a sudden, someone bumps into the back of you, stepping all over the backs of your feet! How would you feel? Angry, right? But then you turn around and see that it's a kindergartener who got away from his mom and is running around, lost and scared, in your school. How would you feel now? You'd probably want to help the little guy, right? So you see, it's not someone bumping into you that made you mad…it was YOUR THOUGHTS about getting bumped that made you mad! You still got bumped, but your thoughts about getting bumped changed when you turned around and saw it was a scared kindergartener. You thought, "let me help him" rather than "that jerk pushed me," and so you felt bad for the kindergartener rather than mad at him. And this is great, great news: if your thoughts cause your anger then you always have total control over your anger. You CAN control your anger. So let's say it all together now…what makes you angry? **YOUR THOUGHTS!**

 # Appendix K: Dear Be Cool! Experts

Advising others is a great way to apply and practice knowledge learned! Because group members are now "experts" on anger management strategies, they will have a chance to help others deal with their anger. Pair up group members and hand out one of the "Dear Be Cool! Experts" scenarios below to each pair. Give pairs 5–10 minutes to use their Appendix K resource, as well as their own ideas, to find a solution for their fellow anger sufferer. Then have each pair read the scenario aloud and tell the group what advice they would give to the angry writer.

Dear Be Cool! Experts,

I have a terrible temper. Whenever someone mean mugs me or looks at me funny, I think they're making fun of me, and this makes me furious! I either yell at them or want to fight. Please help me find a way to control my anger and ignore these looks!

Help, Mean Mugged in Miami

Dear Be Cool! Experts,

Every day there's this kid in my math class who makes fun of me in front of her friends. I've tried to ignore her, but I'm getting really enraged about this issue and I'm afraid I might snap one day! What should I do?

Yours truly, Snappy

Dear Be Cool! Experts,

I got in a fight last week with my enemy, and now we both have to go to the alternative school for a 30-day placement! I know we'll be in the same classroom because there are only a few kids there (I've been there before). My anger keeps getting me in trouble, and I'm afraid this will continue when I have to be in the same classroom as my enemy. What can I do to solve this problem and stay out of trouble?

Sincerely,

Fightin' Mad

Dear Be Cool! Experts,

I REALLY hate going to spend weekends with my dad in New York City. I can't stand his girlfriend who lives with him and bosses me around. Also, it's really hard to switch to a different routine and home every weekend, especially in a city so loud and busy. This situation is making me madder and madder. I used to be able to just keep my feelings to myself, but I can't anymore. What should I do?

From,

The Mad Hatter in Manhattan

Dear Be Cool! Experts,

I have a really bad habit in class: I talk back and get defensive any time a teacher accuses me of something. This happens even when it's my fault! I think I'm so used to getting in trouble at home that I always have an angry answer ready when the teacher calls me out at school. Help!

Sincerely,

Not the Teacher's Pet

Dear Be Cool! Experts,

I'm having a problem with my brother. He goes in my room and gets into my stuff and then when I get mad and yell at him, he goes crying to our mom. My mom likes him better because he's the baby and she always takes his side. How do I handle this annoying kid?

From,

Oh Brother

 # Appendix L: Group Experience Evaluation

Date: _____

Congratulations on completing this Tranquila (Be Cool) group program! Making changes in your life and setting goals for yourself is hard work, but the success you experience as a result of accomplishing goals feels awesome. Please take a few minutes now to reflect on what you've learned in group and then answer the following questions.

1. What have you learned about yourself through our group experience?

2. How will what you have learned affect you in the future?

3. Would you recommend this group to a friend? Why or why not?

4. Which group activity did you find most useful?

5. Which group activity did you find least useful?

6. What did you learn about other people during the group experience?

7. Additional comments:

 # Appendix M: Data Analysis

Data are crucial to showing the importance and relevance of any counseling program. Collecting, and especially compiling, data is never easy and takes time. But no counseling program is complete without these data! Below is how we show our group data, along with some tips and explanations on how to compile the data. It takes us about 2 full days to compile the six data analysis parts after a group has ended, but you can use as many or as few of the parts below in your data reports. We find it is best to wait about 1–2 months after the group has ended before compiling the data in order to get the most complete information.

Part One: Group Title, Date, Number of Participants, and Description

Explanation: In this part, we include the title of the group, the semester and year it occurred, the total number of group members, and a brief description of the group.

Tranquila (Be Cool), Spring 2015

Total Number of Group Members: 7

Tranquila (Be Cool) is a group for students who struggle with expressing their anger in a healthy way. Group members learn about the different healthy ways to manage anger and then each participant sets an anger management goal for themselves to work on during and outside of group sessions. Students continue in the group for six to eight sessions. We also use group techniques such as discussion, role-playing, games, and more to help them achieve their goals.

Part Two: Group Member Evaluations

Explanation: In this part, we include a brief summary of our group member evaluation instrument (Appendix L) and some meaningful group member evaluation quotes showing what they learned in group.

Group members complete a short evaluation during our final group session to evaluate the group experience—what went well, what didn't go well, how the group has helped them, what they still need help with, etc.

Group member responses:

As a result of the group, I learned...

how to handle bad situations.

it (the strategies) made me more calm.

I only get mad because of myself.

I can control my anger.

I'm not the only one with problems.

about how to control my anger.

Part Three: Pre/Posttest Results

Explanation: In this part, we compile the group members' pre/posttest answers into the chart below, using an Excel spreadsheet. Then we highlight the chart in Excel, click on the "Insert" tab in the ribbon of commands, click on "Insert Column Chart," and select the first 2-D Column Chart option; this automatically turns our chart into a graph. Once the graph has been created, you can customize it using one of the design options Excel offers; we keep it easy and simple by using layout 9 from the "Quick Layout" pulldown menu under "Chart Tools > Design."

	Statement 1 – Anger Control	Statement 2 - Strategies	Statement 3 - Emotions	Statement 4 – Anger Causes	Statement 5 – Anger Effects
Pretest: # of Correct (Affirmative) Answers	1	0	5	0	3
Posttest: # of Correct (Affirmative) Answers	5	6	6	6	5

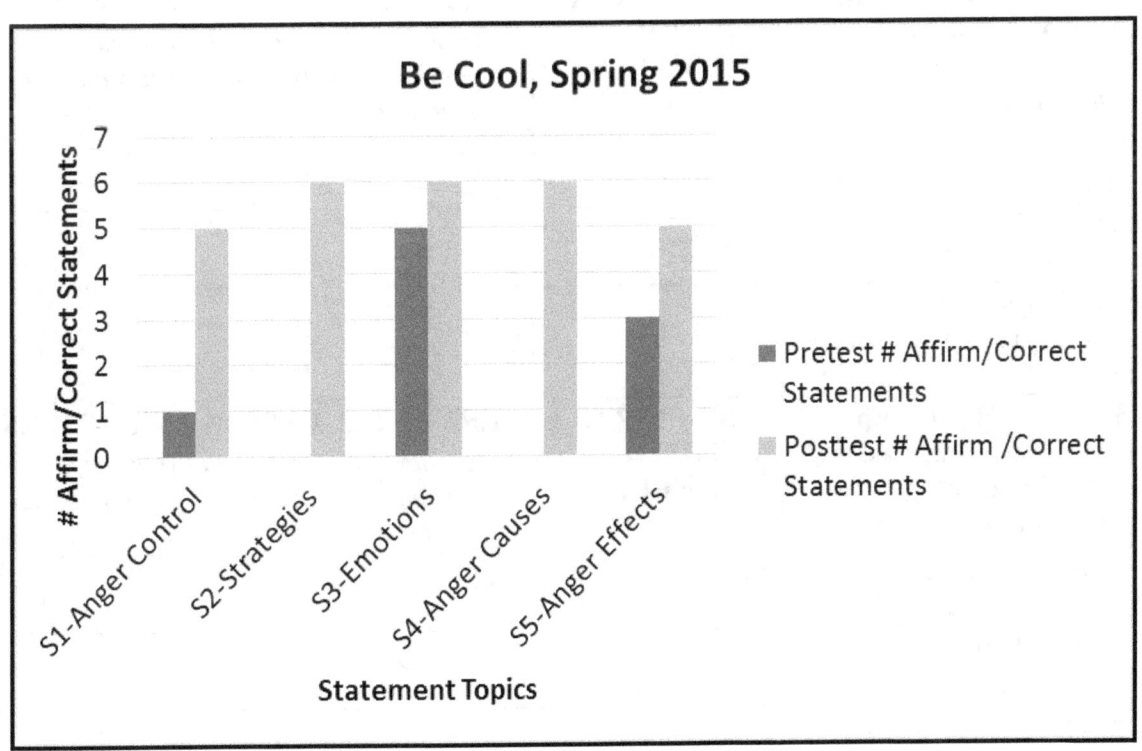

Part Four: Grade Averages

Explanation: In this part, we analyze the grades of all group members for the term before, the term during, and the term after the group sessions. We plug the number of passing grades each group member achieved before, during, and after the group experience into the first chart below. Then we use the data in the first chart to calculate the increases in the number of classes they passed in the second chart. This shows how the group experience has contributed to improved student academic achievement.

	Number of Passing Classes before Group	Number of Passing Classes during Group	Number of Passing Classes after Group
Group member 1	4	5	7
Group member 2	6	7	8
Group member 3	6	6	5
Group member 4	6	2	4
Group member 5	7	7	6
Group member 6	7	7	8
Group member 7	5	5	7

DURING GROUP (compare number of passing classes from before group to during group columns above)	NUMBER OF GROUP MEMBERS	Percentage of GROUP MEMBERS Formula: # members who increased amount of passing classes ÷ total group members = percentage
Members who increased amount of passing classes by 1	2	28%
Members who increased amount of passing classes by 2	0	0%
Members who increased amount of passing classes by 3 or more	0	0%
AFTER GROUP (compare number of passing classes from during group to after group columns above)	NUMBER OF GROUP MEMBERS	PERCENTAGE of GROUP MEMBERS Formula: # members who increased amount of passing classes ÷ total group members = percentage
Members who increased amount of passing classes by 1	2	28%
Members who increased amount of passing classes by 2	3	42%
Members who increased amount of passing classes by 3 or more	0	0

Part Five: Discipline Referrals

Explanation: In this part, we analyze the disciplinary referrals of all group members before, during, and after the group sessions. We plug the number of disciplinary referrals received before, during, and after group sessions into the first chart below, and then we use the data in the first chart to calculate decreases in disciplinary referrals in the second chart. This shows how the group experience has contributed to improved student behavior.

	Number of Disciplinary Referrals before Group	Number of Disciplinary Referrals during Group	Number of Disciplinary Referrals after Group
Group member 1	16	1	3
Group member 2	2	0	0
Group member 3	2 (last year)	0	1
Group member 4	22	3	4
Group member 5	0	0	0
Group member 6	3 (last year)	0	2
Group member 7	7	2	3

DURING GROUP (compare number of disciplinary referrals from before group to during group columns above)	NUMBER OF GROUP MEMBERS	PERCENTAGE of GROUP MEMBERS *Formula: # members who decreased discipline referrals ÷ total group members = percentage*
Members who decreased discipline referrals by 1	0	0%
Members who decreased discipline referrals by 2	2	28%
Members who decreased discipline referrals by 3 or more	4	57%
AFTER GROUP (compare number of disciplinary referrals from during group to after group columns above)	NUMBER OF GROUP MEMBERS	PERCENTAGE of GROUP MEMBERS *Formula: # members who decreased discipline referrals ÷ total group members = percentage*
Members who decreased discipline referrals by 1	0	0%
Members who decreased discipline referrals by 2	0	0%
Members who decreased discipline referrals by 3 or more	0	0%

Part Six: Summary of Data

Explanation: In this part, we analyze all the charts and graphs in parts 3–5 and write a summary that explains the data trends for campus stakeholders.

The pre/posttest bar graph shows that the group members learned the most about the topics of controlling their anger, anger management strategies, and the causes of anger. Most of the group members already knew that anger is a normal human emotion when expressed healthfully, probably due to effective teaching through the Second Step program and through guidance lessons.

During the Tranquila (Be Cool) group, 28% of group members increased the number of classes they passed. After group, 70% of group members increased the number of classes they passed!

During the group, 85% of group members decreased their disciplinary referrals, with one member going from 16 referrals down to 1 referral and another member going from 22 referrals down to 3 referrals!!! Because most group members had few or no referrals (one or less) during the group, it was not possible to collect much after-group disciplinary improvement data, and most of the percentages in this section are low. Also, it is typical for the anger management group members' disciplinary referrals to increase when they don't have weekly opportunities to practice their anger management strategies. Unfortunately, with only two school counselors and a school population of almost 1,000, maintaining an ongoing group support is not possible, even though there are group members who clearly need it.

 # Appendix N: Cool It! Game

Materials: anger management strategies (cut out the strategies on the next page so that each strategy is on an individual slip of paper), decorated box, set of dice, chips (optional)

Directions:

1. Cut out the slips of paper showing the anger management strategies and put them in a box.

2. Have a group member take one strategy from the box and roll the dice.

3. If they roll an even number, they must give an example of a time that they used the strategy and how they felt as they used it. If the group member has never used the strategy, they can describe a situation where they might use it in the future.

4. If they roll an odd number, the group member on their right must give an example.

5. If they roll doubles, the entire group must discuss the strategy and share their experiences with using it.

6. After the first group member has taken their turn, have the next group member take a turn, moving in a clockwise position.

7. Continue playing until everyone has had two or three turns.

8. If group members can handle it, give them a chip each time they are able to give an example of a time they used the strategy or would use the strategy in the future. This really motivates them to rack their brains and talk about their successes with anger management strategies. The group member with the most chips at the end of the game can win a small prize.

www.bilinguallearner.com

Anger Management Strategies

Take time out and relax.	Make a joke out of it.
Count to ten.	Laugh at yourself.
Take five deep breaths.	Tell them to stop in a serious way.
Feel yourself go all rubbery.	Make up with the person.
Walk away from the problem.	Distract yourself by talking to a friend.
Go to a safe place.	Write your feelings on paper.
Ask another student to mediate.	Make a list of bad consequences of you getting angry.
Get help from an adult.	Say you're sorry.
Think about how it's no big deal.	Read your consequences list to calm yourself and control your anger.
Convince yourself to LET IT GO!	Use "I" messages.
Make angry pictures showing how you feel.	Think of something funny about what happened.

 # Appendix O: Group Pass Examples

PASS

Get your lunch at 11:15 and bring it to the counselor's office to eat TODAY at 4th period.

PASS

Come to the counselor's office TODAY at 12:30.

PASS

Come to room 504 TODAY during PE. Please bring this pass.

www.bilinguallearner.com

 # Appendix P: Additional Activities

As mentioned in the recommendations section, these additional activities can be used to extend sessions or as replacement activities during sessions.

Some parts of these additional activities may need modification for very young group members. If necessary, you might read aloud while young group members follow along with their finger. In addition, young group members might dictate to you when necessary (for example with the comics) rather than writing on their own.

Read All About It!

If you have time in your sessions, it is wonderful to add 5–10 minutes of read-aloud time to the beginning of the session. Read-aloud time is especially calming for those who are battling anger issues, and it is also an excellent filler activity as group members are entering your group session during the first five minutes of the session. Below is a list of excellent books that include themes of anger management. Also included are some examples of thought-provoking discussion questions in case you would like to explore the book's themes together through discussion.

Titles

Josh's Smiley Faces: A Story about Anger, by Gina Ditta-Donahue
Hot Stuff to Help Kids Chill Out: The Anger Management Book, by Jerry Wilde
How to Take the Grrrr Out of Anger, by Elizabeth Verdick and Marjorie Lisovskis
Cool Down and Work Through Anger, by Cheri J. Meiners
Angry Octopus, by Lori Lite and Max Stasuyk
I Was So Mad (Little Critter), by Mercer Mayer
The Magic Finger, by Roald Dahl and Quentin Blake
The Outsiders, by S. E. Hinton
Lord of the Flies, by William Golding
A Long Way Gone: Memoirs of a Boy Soldier, by Ishmael Beah (This is an excellent and spellbinding memoir but it is too long and too violent to read aloud in its entirety; however, certain parts can be read to show the damaging power of anger.)

Discussion Questions

- What did you learn from the story?

- Does the main character deal with his/her anger healthfully or unhealthfully? How?

- What anger management strategies does the main character use?

- Do you know anyone in your family who expresses their anger unhealthfully? How do you feel about it?

- What is the problem in the story? Tell me about a problem in your life.

- What is the solution? What kinds of solutions do you like?

This Is How We Do It

Video skits and public service announcements (PSAs) on anger management can be very helpful in showing group members how other people manage their anger in a healthful way. You can follow the video activity steps below to extend your sessions or in place of the role-playing activity in session two or session three until group members get more comfortable with each other and the group experience. To utilize videos with group members, start by giving a brief synopsis of the video and then ask members for ideas on why they are watching this video in group. Next, show group members the discussion questions below (written on chart paper) so they know what to watch for as they view the video.

At the time of this printing, there are no free Spanish language video skits or public service announcements (PSAs) on anger management that show how other people manage their anger in a healthful way. Instead you can type Angry Birds Spanish into an internet search engine and take your pick of various Spanish language cartoons showing the popular characters dealing with anger in both healthful and unhealthful ways.

Discussion Questions

- What anger management strategy did you see or did the person in the video talk about?

- How was the person able to use their anger management strategy?

- What happened as a result of using their anger management strategy?

- What might have happened if the person hadn't use their anger management strategy?

- What other strategies could they have used instead?

Finally, show the video and talk about the discussion questions. Below are some good resources for anger management video skits or PSAs. All of these videos can be found by typing the full titles into a Web search engine or by going directly to the website listed below and typing the title into the website's own search engine at the top of the webpage.

- Kidshealth.org: "Kids Talk About Bullying" (This video is more about bullying than anger; however, it does address a couple of anger issues related to bullying and how to handle both in healthful ways.)

- Kidshealth.org: "Train Your Temper"

- Schooltube.com: "Anger Management PSA"

- Schooltube.com: "Anger Management, Williston Middle School"

- Schooltube.com: "Anger Management"

- Watchwellcast.com: "Anger Management" (This is a video for older group members; it really isn't appropriate for elementary school group members. You can locate it by selecting *All Episodes* at the top of the website.)

Tear It Up

This art activity is a simple, cathartic project that group members can complete fairly quickly. To start, provide group members with various colors of tissue paper. Let them do some healthy venting by tearing the tissue paper into different shapes- strips, little pieces, etc. Then hand out an 8 × 11 piece of cardstock or construction paper to each group member. Members can glue down their torn tissue paper pieces to make pictures showing how they're feeling. Anyone who would like to can present their artwork to the group.

Calming Strategies

Often people can manage their anger very well by using various calming strategies, such as muscle relaxation or breathing exercises. Below is part of a resource from one of our other guides, *The Unstressables*, that describes various calming strategies and how to use them. Hand out the following list of calming strategies to each group member and read it in a round-robin fashion. Then teach and lead the group in practicing each strategy. If you would like more detailed activities with stress management counseling, consider using our group counseling guide, *The Unstressables*, which you can find at **www.bilinguallearner.com** in English or Spanish.

Breathing Backward

This breathing strategy is simple and introduces an opposite way of breathing than we are used to—exhale first, inhale second. Follow these steps to learn the Breathing Backward technique:

1. Purse your lips and hold up one finger.

2. Exhale through your mouth with pursed lips while you hold up one finger.

3. Inhale through your nose while you hold up two fingers.

4. Repeat (exhale breath first, inhale breath second) four more times.

Muscle Makeover

This muscle relaxation exercise can be done anywhere, even sitting at your desk during a test! Follow these steps to learn the Muscle Makeover technique:

1. Sit upright in your chair.

2. Scrunch up your entire face like you just smelled something really bad: eyes squeezed shut, mouth puckered, nose crinkled, etc. Hold for 5 seconds and then let your entire face relax into a calm expression. Repeat four times.

3. Clench your fists as tight as you can and hold for 5 seconds, then release. Repeat four times.

4. Push your arms out at about a 35-degree angle from your body, stretching them and reaching down as far as you can. Hold for 5 seconds and then release to let your arms fall gently at your sides. Repeat four times.

5. Push the soles of your feet into the floor as hard as you can, holding onto your chair or desk for leverage. Hold for 5 seconds and release, relaxing your legs. Repeat four times.

6. Curl your toes inside your shoes as tight as you can, holding for 5 seconds. Then release your toes to lie flat in your shoes. Repeat four times.

Vent It!

This calming strategy lets you share your feelings about and experiences with stress and anxiety with another person by using an "I" message. An "I" message is a calmly spoken sentence where the stressed person tells another person how they feel or what they want beginning with the word "I." Find someone you trust who you know cares about you and start up a conversation about your stress to give yourself a chance to vent! Here are the steps to the Vent It! strategy:

1. Think about why you're feeling stressed.

2. Now think of someone you trust and what that person could do to help you feel less stressed.

3. Use an "I" message to tell that person or a group member how you feel.

4. Now tell that person how they can help you or what you'd like them to do. Sometimes the only thing you need is for them to listen. If that's the case, you can tell them that.

Anger Management Squeeze Bag

If your group members want a stress ball to use as an anger management tool and they like to do craft activities, you can add this fun project to your sessions. With the group, define stress and discuss how it relates to anger. Then brainstorm some ways to handle stress with your group members. Ask them how they might use a stress ball or anger management squeeze ball to manage their anger or combat stress in a way that no one around them would even know they have a stress ball or bag. Give each group member a resealable plastic bag and cotton balls. They should stuff their plastic bag with as many cotton balls as possible and then zip it up. Voila, Anger Management Squeeze Bag! If you work with younger group members, this might be a good time to brainstorm appropriate and inappropriate ways to use their squeeze bag. If you work with older group members, you can hand out colored permanent markers so they can draw anger management designs on their squeeze bag.

It's Comical

Comics are a great way to combine art and anger management. Group members can begin this activity by thinking about their favorite funny experience, movie, joke, or story. Then have them draw a comic depicting this humorous topic. Once they've finished, they can display the comic in a prominent place in their home and think of it anytime they start to feel angry. Sources for blank comics can be found all over the Web; just google "free blank comic" and then take your pick! On the next page is an example I made from an excellent comic creation site called Make Beliefs Comix (**http://www.makebeliefscomix.com/Printables/**). Alternately, if your group members don't have Internet access during the group session, they can cut out the comics in the local newspaper and replace the text with their own text. Group members can also make their own comics by drawing two to four squares, drawing their own comic characters (or using magazine cutouts) within the squares, and finally filling in the dialogue bubbles with their funny experience! If you have time, have the group members do a "comic walk" where they can view and enjoy each others' comics.

KidsHealth

Kidshealth.org is an amazing online resource for kids, teens, parents, and mental health professionals. If you have extra time, you can take advantage of this resource with your group members by reading them "Dealing with Anger" (older group members) or "Taking Charge of Anger" (younger group members). To find these articles, just go to **www.kidshealth.org**, click on the icon for the age group you're working with (kids or teens), and then type the title of the article above into the search engine to navigate right to it. Start this activity by reviewing some anger management strategies with group members, then read the article and ask them a few of the discussion questions below. Next, give group members a virtual tour of both the anger and feelings pages of the website as well as the other health topics, showing them that KidsHealth includes more than just resources on anger management. Finally, give group members a little card with the website URL on it so they can access the site content on their own.

Discussion Questions

- What was the most interesting part of the article?

- What was the most confusing part of the article?

- What did you learn from the article?

- Tell me about someone you know who deals with his/her anger healthfully or unhealthfully.

- What anger management strategies does the article recommend?

- Can people with anger problems change? Tell me about someone you know who changed.

BILINGUAL APPENDICES:

Spanish Translated Activities & Templates

These bilingual appendices can be substituted for their English counterpart with bilingual/ESL students who need the information in Spanish. Since this is a bilingual counseling guide (rather than a Spanish language counseling guide), only the student materials are provided in Spanish; for all counselor instructions or descriptions of activities, you can refer back to the English sessions or English appendices.

Apéndice SB: Antes/Después del Test

Nombre: _____ **Fecha:** _____

<u>Tranquila</u>

Antes del Test Si/No	Declaraciones - Si/No	Después del Test Si/No
	Yo puedo controlar mi enojo.	
	Yo conozco cinco estrategias para calmar mi enojo.	
	El enojo es un sentimiento humano normal.	
	Otras personas o sucesos me enojan.	
	El enojo puede causar enfermedades del corazón o cáncer.	

 # Apéndice SC: Reglas del Grupo & Consecuencias

Las Reglas del Grupo

1. Sólo di cosas útiles.

2. No le cuentes a nadie lo que se dice en el grupo.

3. A su turno sólo habla una persona - no se permiten las charlas a un lado.

4. Usa el baño sólo antes o después de la sesión del grupo.

5. No te burles.

6. No toques las cosas de otra persona.

7. Si llegas tarde, trae un permiso con la hora y firma de un adulto responsable.

Consecuencias

1. Amonestación privada

2. Sales del grupo

 Apéndice SD: Consejos sobre el Enojo

Información importante sobre el enojo

- El enojo es un sentimiento normal.

- Maneras poco saludables de expresar el enojo causan problemas.

- Es fácil enojarse cuando estás cansada o enferma.

- TUS PENSAMIENTOS te enojan - NO otras personas o sucesos.

- El mejor momento para controlar tu enojo es cuando el enojo empieza.

- Si tú no controlas tu enojo, éste puede empeorar.

- Cuando las personas se enojan, pueden lastimarse o lastimar a los demás.

Manejando el enojo

- Dile a alguien cómo te sientes.

- Relájate y respira hondo.

- Aléjate de la situación que enoja.

- Haz ejercicio para calmar tu enojo.

- Tú tienes una opción para expresar tu enojo. Piensa en las diferentes opciones que tienes.

- Tu opción tendrá una consecuencia. Piensa en las consecuencias que tendrán tus acciones.

Vas a tener problemas si

- Rompes algo.

- Golpeas o pateas a personas o a animales.

- Gritas enojada.

- Rompes las reglas en la escuela o el hogar.

 # Apéndice SE: Evaluación del Grupo

Comportamientos	De acuerdo 3	Más o Menos 2	En desacuerdo 1
La líder del grupo sólo habló un poco.			
Los miembros del grupo me escucharon.			
Lo que hicimos en grupo me parece útil/importante.			
Espero que hagamos los mismos tipos de cosas la próxima semana.			

 # Apéndice SF: Estrategias para Manejar el Enojo

¿CÓMO MANEJAS TU ENOJO?
Escoge la estrategia que mejor funcione para ti, para manejar tu enojo.

1. Toma tu tiempo y relájate.
Cuenta hasta 10. Toma 5 respiraciones profundas. Siéntete como si fueras liviana como una pluma.

2. Aléjate del problema.
Ve a un lugar seguro.

3. Escribe o dibuja tus sentimientos en papel.
Haz dibujos o palabras que muestren cómo te sientes.

4. Usa el humor. Haz una broma.
Piensa en algo divertido de lo que te pasó o ríete de ti misma.

5. Piensa de esta manera: "No es gran cosa." Dite: "¡Ya déjalo!"
Decide si el problema vale la pena como para molestarte tanto.

6. Habla sobre el problema.
Dile a la persona cómo te sientes o dile, seriamente, que se detenga y deje de molestarte.

7. Di "lo siento."
Sólo di esto si lo crees en serio.

8. Pide ayuda a un adulto.
O pide a otro estudiante que haga de intermediario.

9. Haz una lista sobre las malas consecuencias que trae enojarte.
Lee la lista para calmarte y controlar tu enojo.

Apéndice SG: Carta de Permiso de los Padres

Fecha _____

Estimados padres:

En la escuela _____, los estudiantes pueden participar en grupos de apoyo con la consejera. Se ha recomendado a su niño/a, _____, participe en el asesoramiento de la escuela. Con su permiso, la consejera va a trabajar con su hijo/a en un grupo sobre _____. Las sesiones no van a interrumpir el programa académico de su hijo/a. La participación en las sesiones de grupo es completamente voluntaria y se respeta la confidencialidad.

La consejera de su hijo/a es la/el Sra./Sr._____.

A veces es necesario y beneficioso que la consejera y el personal escolar (directora, subdirectores, trabajador social, psicólogo, maestros, enfermera, etc.) intercambien información sobre su hijo/a (objetivos, estrategias, avances, etc.). Estos intercambios de información estarán relacionados con las necesidades escolares de su/s hijo/s.

Este permiso es efectivo para el año escolar _____.

Si usted desea que su hijo/a tenga sesiones de grupo con la consejera de la escuela, por favor firme y devuelva este formulario a la oficina de la consejera. Si usted tiene alguna pregunta, puede llamarme a mi oficina: _____.

Gracias,

_____
Consejera Escolar

Doy mi permiso para que _____ pueda participar en un grupo de apoyo con la consejera de la escuela.

_____
Firma del padre/madre

_____
Número de teléfono

 # Apéndice SH: Metas

Meta

Cuando me enoje, prometo que trataré de:

_____.

Los pasos para presentar el éxito de tu meta son:

1. Leer tu meta en voz alta.

2. Dar un ejemplo exitoso cuando hayas alcanzado tu meta.

Apéndice SI: Dibuja tu Emoción

Un dibujo es una buena manera para iniciar una sesión. Aquí tienes dos marcos para los dibujos que vayas a hacer. Para otros dibujos, trata de usar mandalas, que son lindos dibujos que ayudan a las personas a calmarse, sobre todo cuando los pintan (colorean). Busca mandalas gratis en el sitio Pinterest.com.

Cuando estás enojada te sientes muy diferente a cuando estás calmada. Dibuja un dibujo abajo que muestre tu sentimiento cuando estás enojada y tu sentimiento cuando estás tranquila.

ENOJADA

CALMADA

Apéndice SJ: Fragmentos de Lectura sobre el Enojo

¡El enojo causa enfermedades!

El enojo es un sentimiento humano normal que todas las personas sienten. Cuando las personas controlan sus respuestas ante el enojo y expresan el enojo con calma, puede ser una emoción muy útil. Pero, ¿sabías que el enojo podría lastimar a tu cuerpo? Por ejemplo, cuando uno se siente enojado muchas veces por periodos largos de tiempo, puede dañar al corazón, al estómago, los intestinos, y la presión arterial puede subir, entre otros efectos nocivos del enojo mal controlado. Se han realizado muchos estudios durante estos últimos cien años que demuestran que las personas que se enojan frecuentemente tienen más problemas de salud. Estudios específicos demuestran que las personas enojadas tienen el doble de probabilidades de desarrollar enfermedades del corazón y tienen mayores índices de cáncer. Una de las razones para que esto se produzca es que el corazón late más rápidamente y la presión arterial puede aumentar y nuestros cuerpos no pueden manejar estos aumentos si ocurren frecuentemente. Por otro lado, los médicos relacionan al enojo o al estrés con la inflamación que, muchos años después, puede dar como resultado el cáncer. Por lo tanto, si tú te metes en problemas en la escuela, o peleas con otros tu cuerpo, tu salud y tu corazón sufrirán con el enojo.

¿Qué causa el enojo?

Entonces, ¿qué causa tu enojo?

- ¿Tus amigos?
- ¿Tus maestros?
- ¿Tareas difíciles en la escuela?
- ¿Tus padres?
- ¿Tu hermano o hermana?
- ¿Una mirada fea?
- ¿Cuando alguien te grita?

La respuesta es ¡NO! Ninguna de estas cosas puede enojarte, sólo tú puedes enojarte. Tal vez esto suena loco pero vamos a ver un ejemplo. Imagínate: un niño te golpea en la espalda y no ves nada y te caes. ¿Cómo te sientes? Enojada, ¿verdad? Pero después, te das la vuelta y ves que es una niña de kínder que se escapó de su madre, corriendo, asustada y perdida en la escuela. ¿Cómo te sientes ahora? Probablemente tú quieres ayudarla, ¿verdad? Así que no es el golpe lo que te enojó, eran **tus pensamientos** sobre el golpe lo que te enojó. Ya alguien te golpeó, pero tus pensamientos sobre este golpe cambiaron cuando te diste la vuelta y viste a una niña asustada del kínder. Tú pensaste "quiero ayudarla" en vez de "¡esta idiota me golpeó!" y te sentiste triste por la niñita, en lugar de enojarte con ella. Y esto es una buena noticia: si tus pensamientos causan tu enojo, siempre tendrás el control total sobre tu enojo, tú puedes controlar tu enojo. Vamos decirlo todos juntos ahora... ¿Qué te enoja?:

¡Tus pensamientos!

 Apéndice SK: Querida *¡Tranquila!*

Avisar a los demás es una buena manera de aplicar y practicar conocimientos. Cada pareja, en el grupo, puede leer su escenario en voz alta y luego puede decir su consejo al grupo.

Queridas Especialistas de ¡Tranquila!,

A veces tengo un humor explosivo. Cuando alguien me mira de fea o mala manera, creo que se está burlando de mí y ¡esto me da rabia! Por favor ayúdenme a controlar mi enojo y a no hacer caso a las miradas de los otros.

Ayuda,

Una Víctima de las Miradas Feas

Queridas Especialistas de ¡Tranquila!,

Cada día en mi clase de matemáticas hay un niño que se burla de mí, junto con sus amigos. Trato de no hacerle caso pero estoy más y más enojada con esta situación. ¿Qué puedo hacer?

Sinceramente,

Snappy

Queridas Especialistas de ¡Tranquila!,

Me he peleado con mi enemigo hace una semana y ¡ahora los dos tenemos que ir a la escuela alternativa por 30 días! Estaremos en la misma sala porque hay pocos estudiantes allí (ya estuve antes allá). Mi enojo me pone en problemas muchas veces y tengo miedo que esto vaya a continuar porque voy a estar en la misma sala que mi enemigo. ¿Qué puedo hacer para resolver este dilema y para no meterme en problemas?

Sinceramente,

Lucha Libre

Queridas Especialistas de ¡Tranquila!,

Odio pasar los fines de semana con mi padre en la ciudad de Nueva York. No me gusta su novia (que vive con él) y siempre me está dando órdenes. También es muy difícil cambiar de rutina y casa cada fin de semana, especialmente cuando se trata de una ciudad tan ruidosa y ocupada. Esta situación me está enloqueciendo. Solía guardar mi enojo, pero ya no puedo más. ¿Qué puedo hacer?

Sinceramente,

Muchacho en Manhattan

Queridas Especialistas de ¡Tranquila!,

Tengo un mal hábito en clase: Siempre estoy a la defensiva y digo cosas feas cuando un maestro me corrige. ¡Esto sucede incluso cuando es mi culpa! ¡Creo que estoy tan acostumbrada a tener en problemas en mi casa, que cuando la maestra me corrige en escuela siempre le doy una repuesta enojada! ¡Por favor ayúdenme!

Sinceramente,

La Hostil de la Clase

Queridas Especialistas de ¡Tranquila!,

Estoy teniendo un problema con mi hermano. ¡El entra a mi cuarto y hace un desastre con mis cosas! Cuando me enojo y le grito, corre llorando para quejarse con mi madre. Es su favorito, porque es un bebé y ella siempre se pone de su lado. ¿Cómo manejo a este chico tan molesto?

De:

¡Oh Hermano!

Apéndice SL: Evaluación Final del Grupo

Fecha: _____

¡Felicidades por completar este programa sobre *¡Tranquila!* Hacer cambios en la vida es un trabajo muy duro, pero cuando alcanzamos nuestras metas nos sentimos muy bien. Por favor, toma diez minutos para pensar sobre lo que has aprendido en estas sesiones y responde a las siguientes preguntas:

1. ¿Qué has aprendido sobre ti misma en nuestras sesiones?

2. ¿Cómo te afectará este aprendizaje en el futuro?

3. ¿Recomendarías este grupo a tu amiga? ¿Por qué?

4. ¿Qué actividad de nuestras sesiones te pareció más útil?

5. ¿Qué actividad de nuestras sesiones te pareció menos útil?

6. ¿Qué aprendiste sobre otras personas durante nuestras sesiones?

7. ¿Tienes algo más que decir?:

 Apéndice SN: El Juego de ¡Tranquilízate!

Materiales:

Estrategias para el control del enojo (recorta las estrategias que están en la tabla de la siguiente página y colócalas en la caja); dos dados; caja decorada y fichas (opcional).

Instrucciones:

1. Corta las tiras de papel de las estrategias de manejo del enojo y colócalas en la caja decorada.

2. Todas se ubican en círculo. Luego un miembro del grupo retira una estrategia de la caja y tira los dados.

   a. Si tiene un número par, tiene que contar un ejemplo de cuando utilizó esa estrategia y cómo se sintió cuando la usó. Si nunca la ha utilizado, puede hablar de una situación futura donde la podría usar.

   b. Si tiene un número impar, el miembro a su derecha debe dar un ejemplo.

   c. Si le sale doble, todo el grupo puede hablar sobre la estrategia y compartir sus experiencias si la usó alguna vez.

3. Después, el resto de los miembros continúa siguiendo la dirección de las manecillas del reloj.

4. El juego continua hasta que todos hayan tenido entre dos a tres turnos.

5. Si los miembros del grupo pueden manejarlo, entrega una ficha cada vez que den un ejemplo de cuando usaron o usarían la estrategia para el manejo del enojo. Esto realmente los motivará a romperse la cabeza y a hablar de sus éxitos con respecto las estrategias de manejo del enojo. El miembro del grupo con más fichas, al final del juego, puede ganar un premio pequeño.

Estrategias para Manejar el Enojo

Toma tu tiempo y relájate.	Haz una broma.
Cuenta hasta 10.	Ríete de ti misma.
Toma 5 respiraciones profundas.	Dile seriamente que se detenga.
Aléjate del problema.	Habla con un amigo para distraerte.
Ve a un lugar seguro.	Lee la lista de consecuencias para calmarte y controlar tu enojo.
Escribe tus sentimientos en papel.	Haz una lista de las malas consecuencias que trae enojarte.
Haz dibujos que muestren cómo te sientes.	Pide a otro estudiante que intervenga.
Habla sobre el problema.	Pide ayuda a un adulto.
Piensa en algo divertido/chistoso sobre lo que pasó.	Di "lo siento".
Piensa de esta manera: "No es gran cosa".	Decide si el problema vale la pena como para molestarte.
Dite: "¡Ya déjalo!"	Dile un "I" mensaje.

 # Apéndice SO: Pases

PASE

Recoge tu comida a las 11:15 y tráela a la oficina de consejera, para almorzar HOY durante el cuarto periodo.

PASE

Ven a la oficina de consejera HOY a las 12:30.

PASE

Ven a la sala 504 HOY durante tu clase de gimnasia. Por favor, trae este pase.

 # Apéndice SP: Actividades Adicionales

Como se mencionó en la sección de recomendaciones, se trata de actividades adicionales para ampliar o reemplazar ciertas sesiones. Sólo las actividades adicionales que tienen los materiales para los estudiantes han sido traducidas al español. Para encontrar cualquiera de las otras actividades adicionales, con una descripción para el consejero, busque en la versión en inglés: "Additional Activities".

¿De qué Quieres Platicar?

Las pautas para las discusiones sobre os temas que los miembros del grupo quieren charlar, relativas al tema de enojo, son:

- 5–10 minutos (usamos nuestro minutero de grupo)
- Centrado en las soluciones, no en los problemas
- No se usa un nombre específico
- Ayudar todo el tiempo y mantener la seriedad sobre temas del enojo

¡Lee Todo sobre este Tema!

Aquí están los títulos de excelentes libros con temas para el manejo del enojo, así como preguntas que servirán como guía para una discusión posterior.

Libros Sugeridos

Cuando Sofía se enoja, se enoja de veras, por Molly Bang
Keep Your Cool a Child's Solution Book Dealing with Anger (English/Spanish Edition), por Beth Baus
Percy se enoja (I See I Learn), by Stuart J. Murphy
Cálmate y supera la ira, por Cheri J. Meiners
El pulpo enojado, por Lori Lite and Max Stasuyk
Fernando furioso, por Hiawyn Oram
El dedo mágico, por Roald Dahl y Quentin Blake
Rebeldes, por S. E. Hinton
El Señor de las Moscas, por William Golding
Un largo camino: memorias de un niño soldado, por Ishmael Beah

Algunas Preguntas para Iniciar una Discusión

¿Qué aprendiste de la historia?
¿El personaje central expresa su enojo de una manera saludable o perjudicial? ¿Cómo?
¿Cuál estrategia usa el personaje central para manejar el enojo?
¿Hay alguien en tu familia que expresa su enojo de una manera perjudicial? ¿Cómo te sientes respecto a este tema?
¿Cuál es el problema de la historia? Cuéntame sobre un problema que tengas en tu vida.
¿Cuál es la solución? ¿Qué tipo de soluciones te gustan?
¿Hay alguien que cambia en la historia? ¿Conoces a alguien que haya cambiado?

Estrategias para Calmarse

Muchas veces las personas pueden manejar enojo por usar varias estrategias de relajar. En la parte abajo, hay algunas estrategias que los miembros pueden usar para calmarse.

Respira al Revés

1. Frunce tus labios y sostén un dedo en alto.

2. Exhala por tu boca con labios fruncidos cuando tengas un dedo.

3. Inhala por tu nariz cuando tengas dos dedos.

4. Repite (exhala primero, inhala después) cuatro veces más.

¡Músculos, a Relajarse!

1. Siéntate erguida en tu silla.

2. Frunce tú cara como si hubieras olido algo muy feo. Mantén los ojos bien cerrados, la boca fruncida, nariz arrugada, etc. Sigue así por 5 segundos y luego relaja tu cara hasta que obtengas una expresión tranquila. Repite cuatro veces.

3. Aprieta fuerte tus manos y sigue así por 5 segundos, después relaja tus manos. Repite cuatro veces.

4. Extiende tus brazos en línea recta desde tu cuerpo, y extiéndelos tanto como sea posible. Sigue así por 5 segundos y después relaja tus brazos a cada lado. Repite 4 veces.

5. Empuja tus pies hacia el piso lo más fuerte que puedas y agarra el respaldo de tu silla como palanca. Sigue empujando por 5 segundos y después relaja tus piernas. Repite 4 veces.

6. Aprieta tus dedos dentro de tus zapatos lo más fuerte que puedas por 5 segundos. Relaja tus dedos y luego repite 4 veces más.

¡Dile!

1. Piensa por qué estas sintiendo tanto estrés.

2. Ahora, piensa en alguien de confianza- ¿Qué puede hacer esa persona para hacerte sentir menos estresada?

3. Dile a esa persona (o a un miembro de nuestro grupo) cómo te sientes.

4. Ahora, dile a esa persona cómo te puede ayudar o dile lo que te gustaría que haga. A veces la única cosa que se necesita es que alguien te escuche y estando en esta situación, díselo.

KidsHealth.com

Si tiene tiempo adicional con su grupo, puede leer un artículo de Kidshealth.com: "Como Puedo Lidiar con mi Enojo/Dealing with Anger" (para miembros mayores) o "Afrontar mi Ira/Taking Charge of Anger" (para miembros menores). Encuentre estos artículos en **www.kidshealth.org**, y haga "clic" en la edad de su grupo (niños/kids o adolescentes/teens), y después escriba en el "search engine" el título del artículo que quiera usar.

Inicie esta actividad de Kidshealth.com repasando algunas de las estrategias de manejo del enojo, después lea el artículo y formule algunas de las preguntas de discusión que se encuentran en el listado de abajo.

Luego, deles un guía "virtual" de las páginas de sentimientos y de enojo (haga "clic" en el botón "Español" en la columna a la izquierda en la parte inferior de la página). Finalmente, entregue a los miembros una tarjeta con el sitio URL para que puedan usar este sitio por sí mismos.

Preguntas de Discusión

- ¿Cuál es la parte más interesante del artículo?

- ¿Cuál es la parte más confusa del artículo?

- ¿Qué aprendiste del artículo?

- ¿Conoces a alguien que maneje su enojo de una manera saludable o perjudicial?

- ¿Cuál estrategia para manejar el enojo recomienda este artículo?

- ¿Pueden cambiar las personas que tienen problemas con el enojo? ¿Conoces a alguien que haya cambiado?

BILINGUAL LEARNER BOOKS

The Complete ESL for Beginners: Lessons Guide with Activities

ESL for Beginners: Lessons Guide with Activities, Volume One

ESL for Beginners: Lessons Guide with Activities, Volume Two

ESL for Beginners: Lessons Guide with Activities, Volume Three

ESL Express: Lessons Guide for Teaching Beginning English

ESL in the Middle: Lessons Guide for Teaching Intermediate English, Volume One

ESL for Beginners – Culture Explorers

ESL Survival Skills – Exploring US Culture

¡Tranquila! Anger Management Counseling Guide with Spanish/English Activities

Be Cool! Anger Management Group Counseling Sessions Guide with Activities

Where There's a Goal, There's a Way: Individual Counseling Sessions Guide with Activities

¡GOL! Individual Counseling Sessions Guide with Spanish/English Activities

Cope Into Hope: Grief Counseling Guide with Activities

Bilingual Cope Into Hope: Grief Counseling Guide with Spanish/English Activities

Girl World: Girl Empowerment Group Counseling Sessions Guide with Activities

Charla Entre Chicas: Bilingual Girl Empowerment Group Counseling Guide with English/Spanish Activities

The Unstressables: Stress Management Group Counseling Guide with Activities

Relájate: Bilingual Stress Management Group counseling Guide with Spanish/English Activities

Get Your Goal On: Academic Achievement Group Counseling Guide with Activities

***

For information and free downloadable chapters on all Bilingual Learner books, go to www.bilinguallearner.com.

Like our Facebook page and Follow us on Instagram, Twitter or Pinterest to receive info about our other upcoming books.
www.facebook.com/bilinguallearn
www.instagram.com/bilinguallearner
www.pinterest.com/bilinguallearne
www.twitter.com/bilinguallearn

About the Author Stephanie Lerner is a Johns Hopkins University-trained school counselor. She holds a BS in elementary education and an MS in counseling. With more than 15 years in both public and private education, she has Texas certifications in school counseling and bilingual/Spanish education. After traveling the world and teaching in such far off places as Mozambique and Bolivia, Stephanie came home to the United States to be a bilingual counselor and teacher in a high-need public school system. When she's not writing or educating, she enjoys ranch life with her husband and their menagerie of pets—all of whom are bilingual, of course!